Car
Diary

NIC BISHOP

July 21

The house looked such a mess this morning! The living room floor was covered with gear ... piles of warm clothes, bags of food, pots and pans – you name it!

Vivien and I were packing for a canoe trip in the wild, and I didn't want to forget anything – especially the chocolate and peanut butter. Once you're on the river, there are no shops. So if you forget anything, you have to go without!

Luckily, Vivien had made a list of all the things we needed. Life jackets, a tent, maps, sleeping bags ... we checked it all off, and everything was there. But I'm a bit worried. How is it going to fit into our tiny canoe?

bread ✓
cereal ✓
lunches ✓
dried fruit ✓
pasta
peanut butter ✓
chocolate ✓
medical kit ✓
warm clothing ✓
sleeping bags ✓
camera
lenses ✓
film ✓
sketch pad ✓
tent
maps ✓
backpacks ✓
cooker
matches ✓
net

July 24

Today was the first day of the six-day trip. Our supplies *did* fit into the canoe, thank goodness. I didn't want to leave any of that food behind (especially the chocolate!). And the good news is that the weather is meant to be fine for the whole week.

It was great to be paddling up the river at last. The water was so clear, I could see right down to the bottom. Waterweeds swayed lazily in the current, and tiny silver fish glinted in the sunlight.

I watched a **terrapin** swim slowly under the canoe. It looked so peaceful and graceful.

Terrapins spend a lot of time sunbathing on logs.

But things were not peaceful for long. "Moose ahead!" yelled Vivien.

When I looked up, I couldn't believe my eyes! I never realised a **moose** could be so big. It was feeding on the river bank and lifted its head to look at us. I think it was just curious. Maybe it had never seen a canoe before.

The moose is the largest kind of deer in the world. Moose have really long legs so they can walk in deep snow and deep water.

Then I saw a female moose nearby, and there was a small pair of ears poking above the tall grasses. It was a mother *and* her baby. We were really excited. The baby was just a few weeks old, and it trotted off to its mother when it saw us. A mother moose is very protective of her baby, so we didn't hang around for long.

July 25

Today I saw a birch tree on the river bank. It had been eaten almost in half! I could see the tooth marks all over it, and that could mean only one thing – **beavers**.

When a beaver is scared, it slaps its tail on the water to warn other beavers.

I think beavers are amazing animals. Imagine being able to chew through a tree! Lucky for them that their teeth never stop growing, or they'd soon be left with nothing to chew with.

We looked hard for the beavers, but all we saw was a terrapin coming up for a breath of air.

The beavers must have been resting in their lodge. I wouldn't be surprised if they were tired, because we soon came to a huge dam they had built across the river.

We had to get out and pull our canoe over the dam. I was careful not to get any **leeches** in my shoes. Yuck, I hate leeches!

A leech can eat three times its body weight in blood. After that, it can go without food for months.

July 26

We've found a great campsite.
After paddling on the river all day,
we reached a big lake surrounded
by pine and spruce trees.

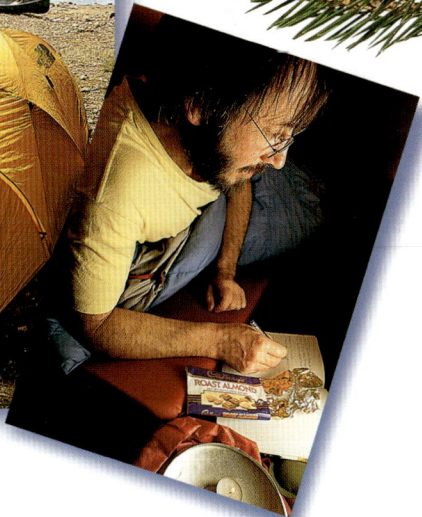

After we'd put up the tent, I went looking for firewood. I nearly picked up a **toad**! It was so still, I thought it was a piece of wood. At first I thought, "Gross!" But when I looked closer, I saw that it was really quite a beautiful animal.

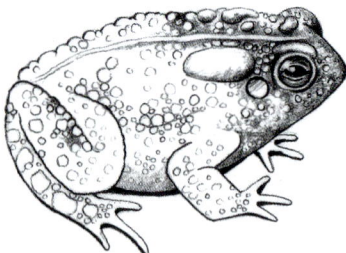

Toads snap up insects with their sticky tongues. Some people think toads look ugly, but they make a beautiful sound when they sing.

I also found a **salamander** under a log and gently touched its moist skin. I read once that salamanders breathe through their skins. Some don't even have lungs.

Salamanders look like lizards, but they are really amphibians, like frogs. They need to live in damp places.

The air got really calm and misty at sunset. **Bullfrogs** started calling from the lake.

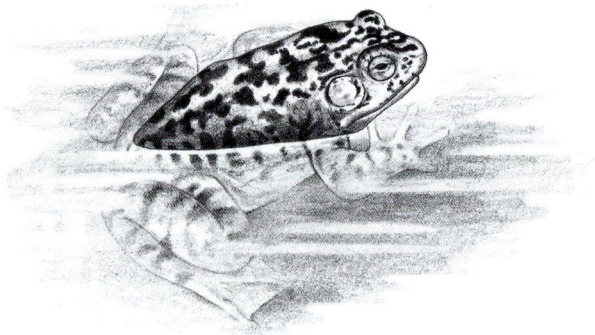

Then I heard a strange sound. It was like a coyote howling, but I knew that it was a **loon**. Another loon called back. Then I heard other loons howling much further away in the darkness. They must have been calling to one another from a lake hidden somewhere in the hills.
It was the most magical sound I'd ever heard.

Before bed, we put all our food into a big bag. We used ropes to haul it up into a tall tree. There are **bears** around here, and if they smell food, they sometimes help themselves.
Bears don't usually mean any harm, but I'd rather not meet one in the wild.

July 27

Last night, I had a real fright. I was just falling asleep when I heard heavy footsteps outside the tent. My heart started pounding.
Was it a bear? I didn't dare look out of the tent or even move! The footsteps sounded so close. Then they headed off into the night.

I was glad no bears were around
when I woke up this morning. But I
could see some loons on the lake.
A pair was fishing together.
I think they had a nest among the
larch trees by the water's edge.

It's hard for a loon to walk on land.
They spend most of their lives in the water.
Before the lakes freeze up at the end of autumn,
loons fly off to spend winter on the sea.

The lake was like a mirror when we set off in our canoe.
A **muskrat** swam by, carrying a bunch of twigs to its house.

Muskrats build "dens" out of piles of weeds and grasses. They eat plants, but they also love to munch on clams.

Then it started to get windy, and we had to paddle harder and harder. A **dragonfly** perched on Vivien's jacket. I think it was glad to have a free ride.

July 28

Swamps are amazing places. There are so many different things living here. We found some strange plants that eat insects. They are called **pitcher plants** because they have leaves shaped like pitchers or jugs.

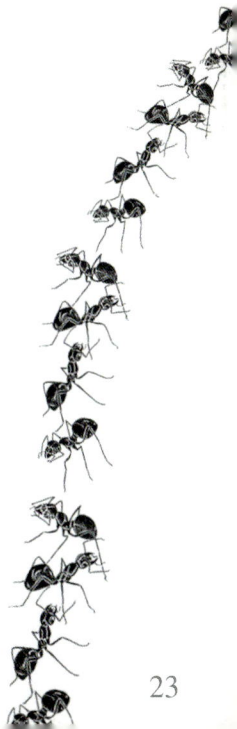

A pitcher plant has lots of tiny bristles, and they all point down. When an insect crawls inside the plant, it can't get back out.

The insect falls into the bottom of the pitcher, and the plant slowly eats it up. I found five **ants** trapped inside one pitcher.

Dragonflies and **damselflies** zipped all around us, hunting for midges and mosquitoes.

Under the water, I could see young dragonflies, called **nymphs**.
They live underwater for up to two years before they turn into adults with wings. I tried to catch a nymph with my net, but it was too fast.

Dragonfly nymphs live underwater for up to two years before they turn into adults with wings.

Instead of a
nymph, I
caught a giant
water bug.
It had a mouth
shaped like a
long tube to
suck the insides
out of other
insects.

Water bugs hide in
the weeds. They
grab other animals
with their strong
front legs. They can
even catch small
fish and frogs.

The best thing we saw was a baby **garter snake**. It was lying by the edge of the swamp, staring into the water. All of a sudden, it pulled out a fish. The snake's mouth stretched wider and wider ... *and wider,* till it swallowed the fish whole!

July 29

It rained last night, and today there were frogs everywhere. Vivien found a baby bullfrog that still had its tail.

When a tadpole turns into a frog, its tail shrinks away. The baby frog grows legs and lungs. Then it can live out of the water.

After breakfast, we had to carry our gear along a short track to another river. That meant carrying all our things, even the canoe. It was hard work. But at least the paddling was easy. It was downstream all the way back to the road.

I think I'm going to miss camping
out and listening to the loons.
I can't wait till our next canoe trip.
Maybe next time we'll see those
beavers.

Index

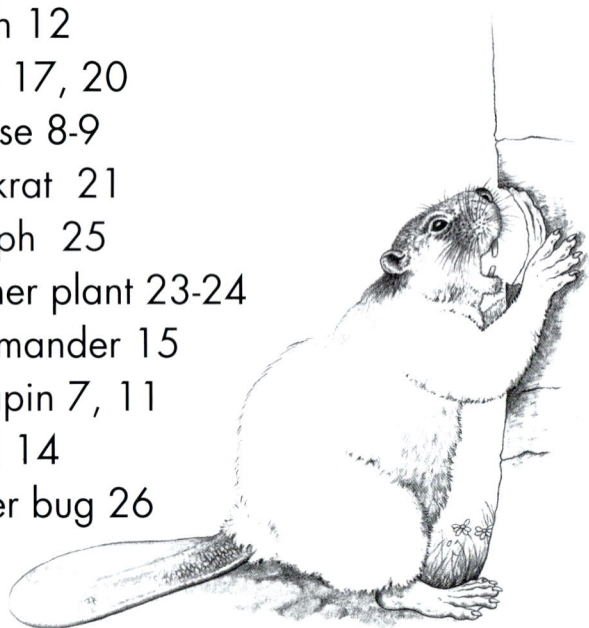